Farrell

by Iain Gray

LangSyne
PUBLISHING
WRITING *to* REMEMBER

Lang**Syne**

PUBLISHING

WRITING *to* REMEMBER

79 Main Street, Newtongrange,
Midlothian EH22 4NA
Tel: 0131 344 0414   Fax: 0845 075 6085
E-mail: info@lang-syne.co.uk
www.langsyneshop.co.uk

Design by Dorothy Meikle
Printed by Ricoh Print Scotland
© Lang Syne Publishers Ltd 2015

ISBN 978-1-85217-253-4

Farrell

MOTTO:
To do good, not to do evil.

CREST:
A greyhound.

NAME variations include:
Ó Fearghail *(Gaelic)*
O'Farrell
O'Farrely
O'Farrel
O'Farelly
O'Farel
O'Farely
O'Farel
O'Farley
O'Farrill
O'Ferrill

Chapter one:
Origins of Irish surnames

**According to an old saying, there are two types of Irish –
those who actually are Irish and those who wish they were.**

This sentiment is only one example of the allure that the
high romance and drama of the proud nation's history holds
for thousands of people scattered across the world today.

It's a sad fact, however, that the vast majority of Irish
surnames are found far beyond Irish shores, rather than on
the Emerald Isle itself.

The population stood at around eight million souls in
1841, but today it stands at fewer than six million.

This is mainly a tragic consequence of the potato
famine, also known as the Great Hunger, which devastated
Ireland between 1845 and 1849.

The Irish peasantry had become almost wholly reliant
for basic sustenance on the potato, first introduced from the
Americas in the seventeenth century.

When the crop was hit by a blight, at least 800,000
people starved to death while an estimated two million
others were forced to seek a new life far from their native
shores – particularly in America, Canada, and Australia.

The effects of the potato blight continued until about
1851, by which time a firm pattern of emigration had
become established.

Ireland's loss, however, was to the gain of the countries in which the immigrants settled, contributing enormously, as their descendants do today, to the well being of the nations in which their forefathers settled.

But those who were forced through dire circumstance to establish a new life in foreign parts never forgot their roots, or the proud heritage and traditions of the land that gave them birth.

Nor do their descendants.

It is a heritage that is inextricably bound up in the colourful variety of Irish names themselves – and the origin and history of these names forms an integral part of the vibrant drama that is the nation's history, one of both glorious fortune and tragic misfortune.

This history is well documented, and one of the most important and fascinating of the earliest sources are *The Annals of the Four Masters*, compiled between 1632 and 1636 by four friars at the Franciscan Monastery in County Donegal.

Compiled from earlier sources, and purporting to go back to the Biblical Deluge, much of the material takes in the mythological origins and history of Ireland and the Irish.

This includes tales of successive waves of invaders and settlers such as the Fomorians, the Partholonians, the Nemedians, the Fir Bolgs, the Tuatha De Danann, and the Laigain.

Of particular interest are the *Milesian Genealogies*,

because the majority of Irish clans today claim a descent from either Heremon, Ir, or Heber – three of the sons of Milesius, a king of what is now modern day Spain.

These sons invaded Ireland in the second millennium B.C, apparently in fulfilment of a mysterious prophecy received by their father.

This Milesian lineage is said to have ruled Ireland for nearly 3,000 years, until the island came under the sway of England's King Henry II in 1171 following what is known as the Cambro-Norman invasion.

This is an important date not only in Irish history in general, but for the effect the invasion subsequently had for Irish surnames.

'Cambro' comes from the Welsh, and 'Cambro-Norman' describes those Welsh knights of Norman origin who invaded Ireland.

But they were invaders who stayed, inter-marrying with the native Irish population and founding their own proud dynasties that bore Cambro-Norman names such as Archer, Barbour, Brannagh, Fitzgerald, Fitzgibbon, Fleming, Joyce, Plunkett, and Walsh – to name only a few.

These 'Cambro-Norman' surnames that still flourish throughout the world today form one of the three main categories in which Irish names can be placed – those of Gaelic-Irish, Cambro-Norman, and Anglo-Irish.

Previous to the Cambro-Norman invasion of the twelfth century, and throughout the earlier invasions and settlement of those wild bands of sea rovers known as the Vikings in the eighth and ninth centuries, the population of the island was relatively small, and it was normal for a person to be identified through the use of only a forename.

But as population gradually increased and there were many more people with the same forename, surnames were adopted to distinguish one person, or one community, from another.

Individuals identified themselves with their own particular tribe, or 'tuath', and this tribe – that also became known as a clann, or clan – took its name from some distinguished ancestor who had founded the clan.

The Gaelic-Irish form of the name Kelly, for example, is Ó Ceallaigh, or O'Kelly, indicating descent from an original 'Ceallaigh', with the 'O' denoting 'grandson of.' The name was later anglicised to Kelly.

The prefix 'Mac' or 'Mc', meanwhile, as with the clans of the Scottish Highlands, denotes 'son of.'

Although the Irish clans had much in common with their Scottish counterparts, one important difference lies in what are known as 'septs', or branches, of the clan.

Septs of Scottish clans were groups who often bore an entirely different name from the clan name but were under the clan's protection.

In Ireland, septs were groups that shared the same name and who could be found scattered throughout the four provinces of Ulster, Leinster, Munster, and Connacht.

The 'golden age' of the Gaelic-Irish clans, infused as their veins were with the blood of Celts, pre-dates the Viking invasions of the eighth and ninth centuries and the Norman invasion of the twelfth century, and the sacred heart of the country was the Hill of Tara, near the River Boyne, in County Meath.

Known in Gaelic as 'Teamhar na Rí', or Hill of Kings, it was the royal seat of the 'Ard Rí Éireann', or High King of Ireland, to whom the petty kings, or chieftains, from the island's provinces were ultimately subordinate.

It was on the Hill of Tara, beside a stone pillar known as the Irish 'Lia Fáil', or Stone of Destiny, that the High Kings were inaugurated and, according to legend, this stone would emit a piercing screech that could be heard all over Ireland when touched by the hand of the rightful king.

The Hill of Tara is today one of the island's main tourist attractions.

Opposition to English rule over Ireland, established in the wake of the Cambro-Norman invasion, broke out frequently and the harsh solution adopted by the powerful forces of the Crown was to forcibly evict the native Irish from their lands.

These lands were then granted to Protestant colonists, or 'planters', from Britain.

Many of these colonists, ironically, came from Scotland and were the descendants of the original 'Scotti', or 'Scots', who gave their name to Scotland after migrating there in the fifth century A.D., from the north of Ireland.

Colonisation entailed harsh penal laws being imposed on the majority of the native Irish population, stripping them practically of all of their rights.

The Crown's main bastion in Ireland was Dublin and its environs, known as the Pale, and it was the dispossessed peasantry who lived outside this Pale, desperately striving to eke out a meagre living.

It was this that gave rise to the modern-day expression of someone or something being 'beyond the pale'.

Attempts were made to stamp out all aspects of the ancient Gaelic-Irish culture, to the extent that even to bear a Gaelic-Irish name was to invite discrimination.

This is why many Gaelic-Irish names were anglicised with, for example, and noted above, Ó Ceallaigh, or O'Kelly, being anglicised to Kelly.

Succeeding centuries have seen strong revivals of Gaelic-Irish consciousness, however, and this has led to many families reverting back to the original form of their name, while the language itself is frequently found on the fluent tongues of an estimated 90,000 to 145,000 of the island's population.

Ireland's turbulent history of religious and political strife is one that lasted well into the twentieth century, a landmark century that saw the partition of the island into the twenty-six counties of the independent Republic of

Ireland, or Eire, and the six counties of Northern Ireland, or Ulster.

Dublin, originally founded by Vikings, is now a vibrant and truly cosmopolitan city while the proud city of Belfast is one of the jewels in the crown of Ulster.

It was Saint Patrick who first brought the light of Christianity to Ireland in the fifth century A.D.

Interpretations of this Christian message have varied over the centuries, often leading to bitter sectarian conflict – but the many intricately sculpted Celtic Crosses found all over the island are symbolic of a unity that crosses the sectarian divide.

It is an image that fuses the 'old gods' of the Celts with Christianity.

All the signs from the early years of this new millennium indicate that sectarian strife may soon become a thing of the past – with the Irish and their many kinsfolk across the world, be they Protestant or Catholic, finding common purpose in the rich tapestry of their shared heritage.

Chapter two:

Resisting the invader

**The name stems from the Irish-Gaelic 'Fearghail',
meaning 'man of valour', and it was certainly with no
small degree of bravery that the Farrells for centuries
defended their ancient homeland of Annaly, in what is
now present day County Longford, in the province of
Leinster.**

They were known as the Princes of Annaly, with the
name of Annaly deriving from their distinguished ancestor
Angall – whose clan was one of the four main clans of the
tribal grouping known as the Conmacne, that traced its
descent back to the celebrated King Fergus MacRoigh and
Queen Maedh.

But it is from Fearghail that the Farrells take their name,
and it was through him that the clan first stamped its name
on the pages of Ireland's colourful and turbulent saga,
fighting at the side of the great warrior king Brian Boru in
one of the most decisive battles in the island's history.

This was the battle of Clontarf, fought about four miles
north of Dublin on Good Friday of 1014.

Late tenth and early eleventh century Ireland was the
scene of vicious inter-clan rivalry as successive clan chiefs
fought for supremacy over their rivals.

It was this disunity that worked to the advantage of the

Norman invaders of the late twelfth century and the Viking invaders of previous centuries.

The period 795 A.D. to 1014 A.D. is known to Irish history as The Viking Tyranny, and it was largely through the inspired leadership of the great Irish hero king Brian Boru that Viking power was diminished, although not completely eliminated.

Boru was able to achieve this by managing to rally a number of other chieftains to his cause – although by no means all.

Among those who did rally to his banner were the warrior Fearghal and his kinsfolk.

Boru, also known as Brian Bóruma and the ancestor of the distinguished O'Brien clan, was a son of Cennetig, king of Dál Cais, in the northern reaches of the province of Munster.

With his battle-hardened warriors known as the Dalcassian knights at his side, Boru had by 1002 A.D. achieved the prize of the High Kingship of Ireland – but there were still rival chieftains, and not least the Vikings, to deal with.

These Vikings, known as Ostmen, had occupied and fortified Dublin in the mid-ninth century and had other important trading settlements on other parts of the island.

Resenting Brian Boru's High Kingship, a number of chieftains found common cause with the Ostmen, and the two sides met in final and bloody confrontation at Clontarf.

Boru proved victorious, but the annals speak of great slaughter on the day, with the dead piled high on the field of battle, while hundreds of Vikings drowned as they sought the safety of their ships.

Among the many dead were not only Brian Boru's three sons, Murrough, Conaing, and Moltha, but also his faithful ally Fearghail, progenitor, or 'name father' of the Farrells.

Boru, meanwhile, had little time to celebrate his victory – being killed in his tent by a party of fleeing Vikings led by Brodar the Dane.

The first to enter the tent had his legs cut off with one sweep of Boru's mighty two-handed sword.

Brodar then struck him a fatal blow on the back of his head with his axe, but he rallied the last of his dying strength to cut off his assailant's head with another sweep of his sword before killing yet another Viking.

Brian Boru and all who fought for him at the battle of Clontarf passed into legend, and the great warrior king was buried in a stone coffin on the north side of the high altar in Armagh church.

The descendants of Fearghail, one of the heroes of the battle, came to dominate what is now Co. Longford with the clan chief, the Lord Annaly, ruling from an imposing stronghold known as Longphuirt Uí Fearghaill, or O'Farrell's Fortress, now the present day bustling town of Longford.

In addition to Longphuirt Uí Fearghaill the Farrells had

another stronghold, known as Móta Uí Fhearghail, or Moat Farrell, in the east of Annaly between the present day communities of Edgeworthstown and Ballinalee.

Nearly two centuries after Brian Boru's victory at Clontarf, with the Farrells having consolidated their hold on their territories, what would ultimately prove to have sown the seeds of the destruction of the ancient native Irish way of life came in the form of invasion from across the Bristol Channel.

Twelfth century Ireland was far from being a unified nation, split up as it was into territories ruled over by squabbling chieftains who ruled as kings in their own right – and this inter-clan rivalry worked to the advantage of the invaders.

In a series of bloody conflicts one chieftain, or king, would occasionally gain the upper hand over his rivals, and by 1156 the most powerful was Muirchertach MacLochlainn, king of the powerful O'Neills.

He was opposed by the equally powerful Rory O'Connor, king of the province of Connacht, but he increased his power and influence by allying himself with Dermot MacMurrough, king of Leinster.

MacLochlainn and MacMurrough were aware that the main key to the kingdom of Ireland was the thriving trading port of Dublin that had been established by invading Vikings in 852 A.D.

Dublin was taken by the combined forces of the Leinster and Connacht kings, but when MacLochlainn died the

Dubliners rose up in revolt and overthrew the unpopular MacMurrough.

Rory O'Connor triumphantly entered Dublin and was later inaugurated as Ard Rí, but the proud Dermott MacMurrough was not one to humbly accept defeat.

He appealed for help from England's Henry II in unseating O'Connor, an act that was to radically affect the future course of Ireland's fortunes.

The English monarch agreed to help MacMurrough, but distanced himself from direct action by delegating his Norman subjects in Wales with the task.

These ambitious and battle-hardened barons and knights had first settled in Wales following the Norman Conquest of England in 1066 and, with an eye on rich booty, plunder, and lands, were only too eager to obey their sovereign's wishes and furnish MacMurrough with aid.

MacMurrough crossed the Irish Sea to Bristol, where he rallied powerful Cambro-Norman barons to his cause.

The mighty Norman war machine soon moved into action, and so fierce and disciplined was their onslaught on the forces of Rory O'Connor and his allies that by 1171 they had re-captured Dublin and other strategically important territories.

Henry II now began to take cold feet over the venture, realising that he may have created a rival in the form of a separate Norman kingdom in Ireland.

Accordingly, he landed on the island, near Waterford, at

the head of a large army in October of 1171 with the aim of curbing the power of his Cambro-Norman barons.

Protracted war between the king and his barons was averted, however, when they submitted to the royal will, promising homage and allegiance in return for holding the territories they had conquered in the king's name.

Henry also received the reluctant submission and homage of many of the Irish chieftains.

English dominion over Ireland was ratified through the Treaty of Windsor of 1175, under the terms of which Rory O'Connor, for example, was allowed to rule territory unoccupied by the Normans in the role of a vassal of the king.

All that had been created was a seething cauldron of discontent as the English grip on Ireland tightened and ambitious and ruthless Anglo-Norman settlers steadily encroached upon the homelands of native Irish clans such as the Farrells.

The Farrells fought a tenacious and largely successful battle to regain lands that had been lost, and by the fifteenth century they had split into two main branches – with the Uí Fhearghail Ban, or White O'Farrell, controlling the north of Annaly and the Uí Fhearghail Bui, or Yellow O'Farrells, controlling the south.

But it was a precarious existence, as the power of the English Crown steadily tightened like a noose around their necks.

Chapter three:

Rebellion and exile

As Ireland groaned under a weight of oppression that was directed in the main against native Irish clans such as the Farrells, an indication of the harsh treatment meted out to them can be found in a desperate plea sent to Pope John XII by a number of Irish chieftains in 1318.

They stated: 'As it very constantly happens, whenever an Englishman, by perfidy or craft, kills an Irishman, however noble, or however innocent, be he clergy or layman, there is no penalty or correction enforced against the person who may be guilty of such wicked murder.

'But rather the more eminent the person killed and the higher rank which he holds among his own people, so much more is the murderer honoured and rewarded by the English, and not merely by the people at large, but also by the religious and bishops of the English race.'

Written appeals proving useless, many native Irish such as the Farrells took up the sword in defence of their ancient freedoms.

Rebellion by landowners against the English Crown's policy of settling, or 'planting' loyal Protestants on Irish land erupted in spectacular and bloody fashion in 1641.

This policy of 'plantation' had started during the reign from 1491 to 1547 of Henry VIII, whose Reformation effectively outlawed the established Roman Catholic faith throughout his dominions.

This settlement of loyal Protestants in Ireland continued throughout the subsequent reigns of Elizabeth I, James I (James VI of Scotland), and Charles I.

In the insurrection that exploded in 1641, at least 2,000 Protestant settlers were massacred while thousands more were stripped of their belongings and driven from their lands to seek refuge where they could.

England had its own distractions with the Civil War that culminated in the execution of Charles I in 1649, and from 1641 to 1649 Ireland was ruled by a rebel group known as the Irish Catholic Confederation, or the Confederation of Kilkenny.

One prominent member of the confederation was Richard O'Farrell, a Capuchin friar.

Retribution for the rebellion came in 1649 when England's 'Lord Protector' Oliver Cromwell descended on Ireland at the head of a 20,000-strong army that landed at Ringford, near Dublin.

He had three main aims: to quash all forms of rebellion, to 'remove' all Catholic landowners who had taken part in the rebellion, and to convert the native Irish to the Protestant faith.

Cromwell soon held the island in a grip of iron, allowing him to implement what amounted to a policy of ethnic cleansing.

His troopers were given free rein to hunt down and kill priests, while 'rebel' estates such as those of the Farrells, were confiscated.

An estimated 11 million acres of land were confiscated and the dispossessed native Irish banished to Connacht and Co. Clare.

An edict was issued stating that any native Irish found east of the River Shannon after May 1, 1654 faced either summary execution or transportation to the West Indies.

Before the seventeenth century was out the final death knell of the ancient Gaelic order was sounded, in the form of what is known in Ireland as Cogadh an Dá Rí, or The War of the Two Kings. Also known as the Williamite War in Ireland or the Jacobite War in Ireland, it was sparked off in 1688 when the Stuart monarch James II (James VII of Scotland) was deposed and fled into exile in France.

The Protestant William of Orange and his wife Mary were invited to take up the thrones of Scotland, Ireland, and England – but James still had significant support in Ireland.

His supporters were known as Jacobites, and among them was Ceadaigh O'Farrell.

Following the arrival in England of William and Mary from Holland, Richard Talbot, 1st Earl of Tyrconnell and James's Lord Deputy in Ireland, assembled an army loyal to the Stuart cause.

The aim was to garrison and fortify the island in the name of James and quell any resistance.

Londonderry, or Derry, proved loyal to the cause of William of Orange, or William III as he had become, and managed to hold out against a siege that was not lifted until July 28, 1689.

James, with the support of troops and money supplied by Louis XIV of France, had landed at Kinsale in March of 1689 and joined forces with his Irish supporters.

A series of military encounters followed, most notably James's defeat by an army commanded by William at the battle of the Boyne on July 12, 1689.

Among the Jacobite dead was Ceadhaigh O'Farrell.

James fled again into French exile, never to return, while another significant Jacobite defeat occurred in July of 1691 at the battle of Aughrim – with about half their army killed on the field, wounded, or taken prisoner.

The Williamite forces besieged Limerick and the Jacobites were forced into surrender in September of 1691.

A peace treaty, known as the Treaty of Limerick followed, under which those Jacobites willing to swear an oath of loyalty to William were allowed to remain in their native land.

Those reluctant to do so were allowed to seek exile on foreign shores – but their ancient homelands were lost to them forever.

Among the Farrells who sailed into exile were the three sons of Ceadaigh O'Farrell, who found refuge in France.

Born in 1726 in Burgundy, France, Francis Thurot

O'Farrell was the grandson of a Captain O'Farrell who had settled in France in the wake of the Treaty of Limerick.

Fiercely proud of his Irish roots he was commissioned into the French naval service while England and France were at war.

In 1760 he was serving on a French frigate that managed against all the odds to break through an English naval blockade of Belfast Lough, but he was killed only a short time later when the frigate came under the fire of a British naval squadron.

A further flight overseas occurred following an abortive rebellion in 1798, while Farrells were among the many thousands of Irish who were forced to seek a new life many thousands of miles from their native land during the famine known as The Great Hunger, caused by a failure of the potato crop between 1845 and 1849.

But Ireland's loss of her sons and daughters proved in many cases to be the advantage of those nations in which they settled.

Chapter four:
On the world stage

Generations of Farrells have excelled, and continue to excel, in a colourful range of pursuits – with a significant number achieving fame as stars of stage and screen.

Born in 1976 in the Castleknock district of Dublin, **Colin Farrell** is the Irish actor whose first screen appearances were on the popular BBC television drama *Ballykissangel*, from 1998 to 1999.

By 2000 he had come to international notice for his role in *American Outlaws*, while a succession of further films, including the 2001 *Phone Booth*, the 2002 *Minority Report*, the 2003 *Alexander*, the 2005 *Miami Vice* and the 2006 *Ask the Dust* firmly established him as a major Hollywood star.

He also starred in the 2007 *Cassandra's Dream* while, at the time of writing, he is set to star in *In Bruges*, slated for release in 2008.

Born in 1901 in Walpole, Massachusetts, **Charles Farrell** was both a noted film and television actor who first achieved fame during the silent era of the 1920s, starring beside the actress Janet Gaynor in a series of films including the 1927 *Seventh Heaven*, the 1928 *Street Angel* and the 1929 *Lucky Star*.

By the mid-1950s he was hosting his own American television programme, *The Charles Farrell Show*, while he also starred in the '50s television series *My Little Margie*.

Farrell, who died in 1990, has two stars on the Hollywood Walk of Fame – for his contributions to motion pictures and television.

The archetypal fast-talking brassy blonde, **Glenda Farrell** was the American actress born in Enid, Oklahoma, in 1904.

Her career treading the boards began with a theatre company at the tender age of seven, while her first screen contract was secured at the age of 27.

One of her most famous roles was in the 1931 *Little Caesar*, starring beside Edward G. Robinson while she also starred in a further succession of films including the 1932 *I Am a Fugitive from a Chain Gang* and, a year later, *Mystery of the Wax Museum*.

Promoted by the Warner Bros. studios of being able to deliver to camera an astonishing 400 words in 40 seconds, she starred in her own film series, *Torchy Blane, Girl Reporter*.

She won an Emmy Award for her work on the American medical drama *Ben Casey* eight years before her death in 1971, while she also has a star on the Hollywood Walk of Fame.

Not many Farrells in particular or people in general can boast a planetary body named in their honour, but American actress **Terry Farrell** certainly can.

Born in 1963 in Cedar Rapids, Iowa, the former fashion model is best known for her roles in the television series

Becker and *Star Trek: Deep Space Nine* – and it was through her role in the latter that the asteroid **26734Terryfarrell** was named in her honour by its discoverer, William Kwong Yu Yeung, in 2001.

Born in 1955 in Essex, England, **Nicholas Farrell** is the British stage, film, and television actor who appeared in the 1981 movie *Chariots of Fire* and who has since appeared in a number of popular British television dramas that include Agatha Christie's *Poirot*, *Midsomer Murders*, *Foyle's War*, and *Casualty*.

Also on the screen **Mike Farrell**, born in 1939 in St. Paul, Minnesota, is the American actor best known for his role as Captain B.J. Hunnicutt in the hugely popular television series *M*A*S*H*, between 1975 and 1983.

In more recent times he has starred in the equally popular television series *Desperate Housewives* and *Providence*.

His former wife is the American actress **Judy Farrell**, born in 1938, and who also made a number of appearances on *M*A*S*H*.

One Farrell with a particularly interesting career was the American actor **Timothy Farrell**, born Timothy Sperl in 1922 and who died in 1989.

In addition to working as a bailiff for the Los Angeles Sheriff's Department he also starred in a number of sleazy and low budget movies such as *Girl Gang*, *Jail Bait*, and *The Violent Years*.

On an entirely different stage from that on which Timothy Farrell performed, **Suzanne Farrell**, born Roberta Sue Ficker in Cincinnatti in 1945, is one of the most acclaimed ballerinas of her age.

A dancer at one time for the legendary choreographer George Balanchine, she joined the New York City Ballet in 1961. The recipient of numerous awards, including an American National Medal of the Arts, she started her own ballet company in 2000.

Recognised as one of the founders of Canada's alternative comedy scene, **Mark Farrell**, born in 1968, is the comedian and writer and executive producer for the popular television show *This Hour Has 22 Minutes*.

In the world of music **Eileen Farrell**, born in 1920 in Willimantic, Connecticut, was the renowned American opera and concert singer who was a regular soloist with the New York Philharmonic throughout the 1960s.

The talented soprano died in 2002.

Born in 1949 in Aruba, in the Leeward Islands, **Bobby Farrell** is the musician best known as the male performer in the 1970s popular band Boney M.

Ciarán Farrell, born in 1969 in Dublin, is the Irish composer who studied under the famed Italian film composer Ennio Morricone. His many works include compositions for the Irish Modern Dance Theatre.

Better known as Phoenix, **Dave Farrell**, born in 1977 in Plymouth, Massachusetts, is the bassist for the alternative rock band Linkin Park, while **Gail Farrell**, born in 1947 in Salinas, California, is the singer and songwriter who first rose to fame as a member of the American television musical variety programme *The Lawrence Welk Show*.

From the world of music to the world of architecture, **Sir Terry Farrell**, born in 1939 in Sale, Cheshire, is the leading British exponent of high-tech and post-modernist architecture and whose designs include the headquarters at Vauxhall Cross, London, of Britain's foreign intelligence service M.I.6.

Born in 1827, **Sir Thomas Farrell** was the Irish sculptor whose many works grace the city of Dublin.

In the world of literature **James T. Farrell**, born in 1904 in Chicago and who died in 1979, was the journalist, short story writer and novelist who wrote of the lives and times of the working class Irish-Americans of his native city.

His most famous work is the *Studs Lonigan* trilogy of novels, made into a film in 1960.

Born in Liverpool in 1935 James Gordon Farrell, better known as **J.G. Farrell**, was the British novelist and author of the acclaimed *Empire Trilogy – Troubles*, *The Siege of Krishnapur*, and *The Singapore Grip* – that dealt with the effects of British colonial rule.

Ireland had become his home since he moved there with his parents at the age of twelve – and it was here that he died in 1979 in a drowning accident while angling in Bantry Bay.

One of the many classic Hollywood movies is *Whatever*

Happened to Baby Jane? released in 1962 with Bette Davis in the title role.

The film was based on a novel penned two years earlier by the American short story writer, novelist and screenwriter **Henry Farrell**, born Charles Farrell Myers in California in 1920, and who died in 2006.

Farrell also co-wrote the screenplay for the 1964 *Hush … Hush, Sweet Charlotte*, starring Bette Davis and Olivia de Havilland and based on his story *Whatever Happened to Cousin Charlotte?*

The script earned Farrell and co-writer Lukas Heller an Edgar Award from the Mystery Writers of America for Best Motion Picture Screenplay.

In the highly competitive world of sport **John Farrell**, born in 1906 and who died in 1994, was the American speed skater and coach who took the bronze medal at the 1928 Winter Olympics and who was inducted into the National Speedskating Hall of Fame in 1971.

On the rugby pitch **Andy Farrell**, born in Wigan in 1975, is the English rugby union and former rugby league player who was awarded an Order of the British Empire (O.B.E.) in 2004 for his services to the game, while in the game of field hockey **Renita Farrell**, born in 1972 in Townsville, Queensland, is the former Australian player who was a member of the gold-winning Australian Women's Hockey Team at both the 1996 and 2000 Summer Olympics.

In baseball Richard Farrell, better known as **Turk Farrell**, who was born in 1934, was the renowned American right-handed pitcher who died in a car accident in 1977.

Born in White Plains, New York, in 1901 **Johnny Farrell** was the professional golfer who played for the United States in the first three Ryder Cups (1927, 1929, and 1931) and who won the U.S. Open in 1928. He died in 1988.

In the world of politics **General Edelmiro Farrell**, born in 1887 in Avallaneda, Argentina, was the Argentinian soldier who served as president of the nation between 1944 and 1946.

Another famous Farrell with a military connection was **John Farrell**, born in 1826 in Dublin and who, as a sergeant in the 17th Lancers (Duke of Cambridge's Own), British Army, was awarded the Victoria Cross – the highest award for gallantry for British and Commonwealth forces.

This was on October 25, 1854 during the heroic but abortive Charge of the Light Brigade against Russian guns at Balaclava, during the Crimean War.

His horse was killed under him during the charge and, amidst a storm of shot and shell, he and another sergeant helped to move two severely wounded comrades out of the range of the guns.

Later promoted to Quartermaster-Sergeant, he was killed in action nearly two years later at Secunderabad, in India.

Key dates in Ireland's history from the first settlers to the formation of the Irish Republic:

circa 7000 B.C.	Arrival and settlement of Stone Age people.
circa 3000 B.C.	Arrival of settlers of New Stone Age period.
circa 600 B.C.	First arrival of the Celts.
200 A.D.	Establishment of Hill of Tara, Co. Meath, as seat of the High Kings.
circa 432 A.D.	Christian mission of St. Patrick.
800-920 A.D.	Invasion and subsequent settlement of Vikings.
1002 A.D.	Brian Boru recognised as High King.
1014	Brian Boru killed at battle of Clontarf.
1169-1170	Cambro-Norman invasion of the island.
1171	Henry II claims Ireland for the English Crown.
1366	Statutes of Kilkenny ban marriage between native Irish and English.
1529-1536	England's Henry VIII embarks on religious Reformation.
1536	Earl of Kildare rebels against the Crown.
1541	Henry VIII declared King of Ireland.
1558	Accession to English throne of Elizabeth I.
1565	Battle of Affane.
1569-1573	First Desmond Rebellion.
1579-1583	Second Desmond Rebellion.
1594-1603	Nine Years War.
1606	Plantation' of Scottish and English settlers.

1607	Flight of the Earls.
1632-1636	Annals of the Four Masters compiled.
1641	Rebellion over policy of plantation and other grievances.
1649	Beginning of Cromwellian conquest.
1688	Flight into exile in France of Catholic Stuart monarch James II as Protestant Prince William of Orange invited to take throne of England along with his wife, Mary.
1689	William and Mary enthroned as joint monarchs; siege of Derry.
1690	Jacobite forces of James defeated by William at battle of the Boyne (July) and Dublin taken.
1691	Athlone taken by William; Jacobite defeats follow at Aughrim, Galway, and Limerick; conflict ends with Treaty of Limerick (October) and Irish officers allowed to leave for France.
1695	Penal laws introduced to restrict rights of Catholics; banishment of Catholic clergy.
1704	Laws introduced constricting rights of Catholics in landholding and public office.
1728	Franchise removed from Catholics.
1791	Foundation of United Irishmen republican movement.
1796	French invasion force lands in Bantry Bay.
1798	Defeat of Rising in Wexford and death of United Irishmen leaders Wolfe Tone and Lord Edward Fitzgerald.

1800	Act of Union between England and Ireland.
1803	Dublin Rising under Robert Emmet.
1829	Catholics allowed to sit in Parliament.
1845-1849	The Great Hunger: thousands starve to death as potato crop fails and thousands more emigrate.
1856	Phoenix Society founded.
1858	Irish Republican Brotherhood established.
1873	Foundation of Home Rule League.
1893	Foundation of Gaelic League.
1904	Foundation of Irish Reform Association.
1913	Dublin strikes and lockout.
1916	Easter Rising in Dublin and proclamation of an Irish Republic.
1917	Irish Parliament formed after Sinn Fein election victory.
1919-1921	War between Irish Republican Army and British Army.
1922	Irish Free State founded, while six northern counties remain part of United Kingdom as Northern Ireland, or Ulster; civil war up until 1923 between rival republican groups.
1949	Foundation of Irish Republic after all remaining constitutional links with Britain are severed.